The Power of "I AM"

by Holly Roberts Merrell
Illustrations by Galih Winduadi

Copyright © 2019 by Holly Roberts Merrell
Illustrations: Galih Winduadi

All rights reserved. No part of this book may be reproduced by any mechanical, photographic, or electronic process, or in the form of a phonographic recording; nor may it be stored in a retrieval system, transmitted, or otherwise be copied for public or private use--other than for "fair use" as brief quotations embodied in articles and reviews without prior written permission of the publisher. The intent of the author is only to offer information of a general nature to help you in your quest for emotional and spiritual well-being. In the event you use any of the information in this book for yourself, the author assumes no responsibility for your actions.

Library of Congress Control Number: 2020902160

ISBN: 978-1-951982-04-1
Digital ISBN: 978-1-951982-05-8

Most of us don't realize how powerful our words are; especially the two simple words "I AM."
Because of how powerful these words are, it is very important that we use them carefully. Whenever we use the words "I AM," we are either empowering or limiting ourselves. The words that follow are powerful too. Together they bring about our experiences in life and help to shape our future. To have positive events happen in our lives, we need to think and speak positively. This is done by using positive words. Read through this book and recognize all of the different ways that you have been using the words "I AM." Carefully choose your words and watch your life get a little better each and every day.

Did you know that two of the most powerful words in the world are "I AM"? But what really makes them powerful are the words that follow…

You see...

the words that follow
and the way that we feel
create what we experience,
they actually become real.

The more you say them,
the more they'll sink in,
they'll gain more power
and they'll help you to win.

But it works both ways,
for the good and the bad.

So you can choose to say "I am happy" or you can choose to say "I am sad."

If you say to yourself
"I am stupid" or "I am dumb,"

do you feel good inside
or do you feel like you're scum?

You can't say bad things
and expect to feel good.
If you think you can do this,
then you've misunderstood.

You see, the words "I AM," spoken in thought or in word, they don't go unnoticed, they're always heard.

You may think they're just words
and they don't mean a lot,
but they have much more power
than you've ever thought.

You see...
Our thoughts, feelings, and words,
are actually the source
of what happens in life.
They determine our course.

I grew up not knowing
the power I had,
that I could determine
whether I was happy or sad.

I used the "I AM's"
but in the wrong way.
Here are some "I AM's"
that I used to say...

"I am worthless, I am scared,
and I don't fit in.
I am not as good,
as her or him.

I am ugly, I am bashful,
I am shy and alone...... "
Oh how I wish
these things I had known.

But now that I've learned them,
I've made a big change.
And the things that I want
are actually in range.

Life will have many ups,
but it will still have its downs.
We'll have many smiles
and we'll have many frowns.

Bad things will happen,
that's just a fact.
But we still get to choose
just how we'll react.

Don't forget there is power
behind your words and your thoughts.
And remember that you
are the one calling the shots.

It's your life you're living,
and you get to choose
by your thoughts and your words
whether you win or you lose.

So say "I am awesome,
amazing and cool!"
These two words "I AM"
are a powerful tool!

But when used the wrong way
they don't come from the heart.
And these two simple words
can tear you apart.

So apply what I've taught
and do your best to remove
all the negative words,
and your life will improve.

If you need some ideas
about words you can use,
in these next pages I'll give you,
some helpful clues.

You can use these ones
or think of your own,
or put them together,
and your list will have grown.

There's no right answer,
just give it a try.
You can pick ones you like,
you get to decide.

- I Am Joyful
- I Am Healthy
- I Am Important
- I Am Handsome
- I Am Blessed
- I Am Loveable
- I Am Valuable
- I Am Thankful
- I Am Unique
- I Am Amazing
- I Am dedicated
- I Am Helpful
- I Am Courageous
- I Am Honest
- I Am Priceless
- I Am Happy
- I Am Brave
- I Am Dependable
- I Am Calm
- I Am a good friend
- I Am thoughtful
- I Am a good listener
- I Am Generous
- I Am Confident
- I Am Creative
- I Am Strong
- I Am Respectful
- I Am Positive

- I Am Adored
- I Am Bold
- I Am Brilliant
- I Am Gorgeous
- I Am Cool
- I Am appreciated
- I Am Cheerful
- I Am Clear
- I Am Content
- I Am Cherished
- I Am Focused
- I Am Fabulous
- I AM EXTRAORDINARY
- I Am Decisive
- I Am Trusting
- I Am Terrific
- I Am Wise
- I Am Wonderful
- I Am Fun
- I Am Enthusiastic
- I Am Unlimited
- I Am Magnificent
- I Am Fabulous
- I Am Glowing
- I Am Playful
- I Am Vibrant
- I Am Hopeful
- I Am Inspired

I Am Awesome   I Am Beautiful

I Am Smart   I Am Kind

I Am Special   I Am Funny

I Am Energized   I Am Empowered

I Am Loving   I Am Excited

I Am Powerful   I Am Optimistic

I Am Tender   I Am Worthy

I Am Precious   I Am Whole

I Am Delightful   I Am Succesful

Now use these "I AM's,"
to make your life great.
Change your "I AM's"
before it's too late.

Books by Holly Roberts Merrell...

To learn more about the author and more in depth detail of her personal experiences regarding her books, please visit hollyrobertsmerrell.com.

www.ingramcontent.com/pod-product-compliance
Lightning Source LLC
Chambersburg PA
CBHW041818040426
42452CB00001B/15